# A Gray, Rainy Day

by Dennis Fertig
illustrated by Kersti Frigell

Core Decodable 77

Bothell, WA • Chicago, IL • Columbus, OH • New York, NY

**MHEonline.com**



Send all inquiries to:
McGraw-Hill Education
8787 Orion Place
Columbus, OH 43240

ISBN: 978-0-02-132172-8
MHID: 0-02-132172-8

Printed in Canada.

9 10 11 12 KOD 24

"Will you play for us?" asked Kay.

"I will play on a gray, rainy day," said Jay.

Kay liked to hear Jay play.
Kay had a way to make Jay play.

Kay made a gray painting.
Then Kay fixed the hose to spray.

Kay set up the gray painting.
The hose sprayed.

Kay went back to find Jay.
"It is gray and rainy!" said Kay.

"I will play," said Jay.

"I like to play when it is rainy and gray."